i

Automated and Validated Data Collection

Automated and Validated Data Collection

Jeffrey Lush – bapSolution.com

Jeffrey Lush – bapSolution.com
2018

First Printing: Automated and Validated Data Collection - 2018

ISBN 978-0-359-17050-0

bapPress
bapSolution.com

Contents

Introduction

What makes **BAP** unique in an industry flooded with cybersecurity solutions? *Simple-* **BAP** is Accountable Security, developed with the end state in mind, making

Cyber and Compliance easier, validated and accountable.

The book is complete with a screen shot at the top of each page, followed by insight related to the screen shot and concludes with the actions needed. Although the book is very focused on how BAP completes the process, the **"insight"** section of each page provides information for any reader to leverage when building a validated data collection process, with or without BAP software. You will be surprised at the value BAP brings to the collection of information in an organized, validated and accountable manner.

The chapters are organized to walk the reader through the process from building the interview (two examples of technical and non-technical interviews), to compiling the efforts with bapStrategy, to sharing the interview with other bapFrameworks. We then import the interview as a user, complete the interview and submit the results to the requestor. Our last step returns to the requestor to collect the results and produce a report. This book walks through the bapEnterprise product, please see other bapPress books for going instruction on accomplishing the same tasks using bapCloud.

BAP leverages existing cyber investments, augmenting the tools and information collected to bridge the gap between real-time threat detection and an organization's cyber standards, policy, and compliance. Compliance requires accountability to rules and procedures; **BAP** enables success.

It's as easy as BAP.

Validate data collection
-bapInterview

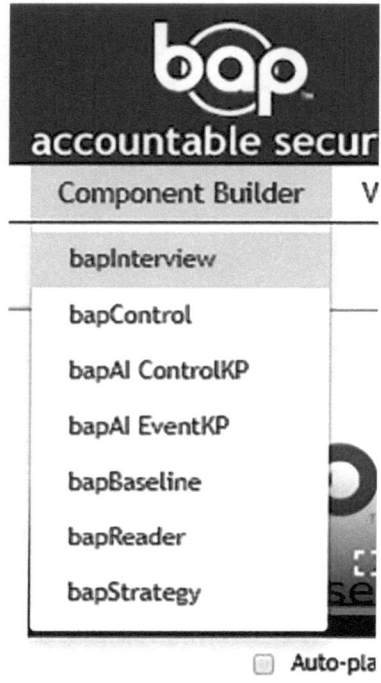

Insight

bapInterview allows you to create automated data calls. The following chapter will go through each screen and provide insight and actions you can take. Please take a few minutes to follow-along through the chapter and explore the many options available. Then go back and create.

Act

1. Choose **Component Builder** from the menu found in the upper left part of the screen.

2. Choose **bapInterview** from the drop-down menu

Create
bapInterview
based on control
or baseline

Create a new
bapInterview

Edit a
bapInteview

Insight

We are now at the main selection screen. Let's start with understanding each of the selections on the screen.

1. Create bapInterview is based on control or baseline: bapInterview allows you to create an interview based on a specific control, a baseline (which is a collection of controls) or an interview that is "non-technical" that are any questions you desire. If you select this option, you will need to have at least one control or one baseline within your BAP framework that you would like to build the interview based upon. You can create "non-technical" questions as part of the interview as well. See chapter 2 if you would like to build an interview based upon a control or a baseline.

2. Create a bapInterview: you will choose this option if you would like to create an interview that is not dependent upon a control or a baseline within your framework. This option is frequently selected to create "data calls"/automated and validated data collection.

3. Edit a bapInterview: this option allows you to edit existing or imported interviews within your framework.

Act

1. Choose one of the options above. For the following pages of this chapter, we have selected "Edit a bapInterview".

Name of the bapInterview to search for   ☐ **Search only disabled components**

▲ bapInterview Name	Last Modified	Status
4.2.3 identification, authentication, and access control v1 by Jeffrey Lush	10/11/2018 00:36	Enabled
4.2.3 identification, authentication, and access control-1 v1 by Jeffrey Lush	10/11/2018 00:42	Enabled
4.2.3-identification, authentication and access control-2 v1 by Jeffrey Lush	10/11/2018 00:45	Enabled
4.2.3-identification, authentication, and access control-4 v1 by Jeffrey Lush	10/11/2018 00:48	Enabled
4.2.3-identification, authentication, and access control-5 v1 by Jeffrey Lush	10/11/2018 00:49	Enabled
4.2.3-identification, authentication, and access control-6 v1 by Jeffrey Lush	10/11/2018 00:50	Enabled
4.2.3-identification, authentication, and access control-7 v1 by Jeffrey Lush	10/11/2018 00:51	Enabled
4.2.3-identification, authentication, and access control-8 v1 by Jeffrey Lush	10/11/2018 00:52	Enabled
4.2.3-identification, authentication, and access control-9 v1 by Jeffrey Lush	10/11/2018 00:53	Enabled
4.2.4-audit, alerting, malware, and incident response-1 v1 by Jeffrey Lush	10/11/2018 00:55	Enabled

Showing 1 to 10 of 66 bapInterviews   Previous   1   2   3   4   5   6   7   Next

Insight

We have selected "Edit a bapInterview". Listed are all the interviews that are available within this framework. Note you have the name of the interview, the version of the interview, the author of the interview, the date of the last edit, and the status.

Status can either be enabled or disabled. By default, many of the components like the interview will be enabled. If you would like to modify the status, choose the tools option, choose component maintenance, choose the correct tab, and choose to enable the component, in this example the interview. Please see additional instruction on enabling and disabling components.

Act

1. Choose the interview you would like to edit.

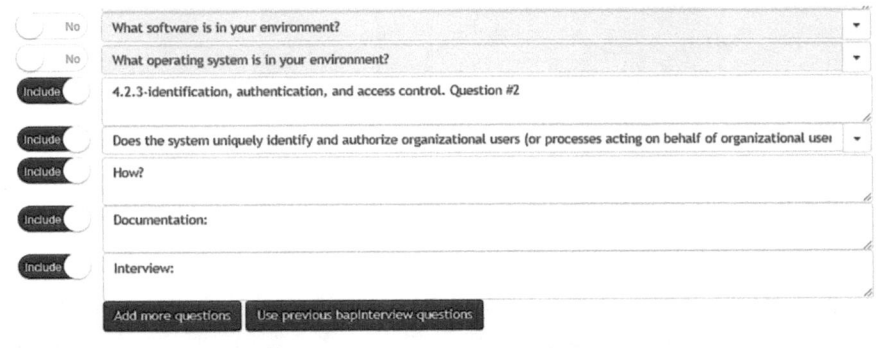

Insight

Listed are some default questions and questions that have been selected previously for this interview. The toggle button will allow you to include or not include the question within your interview.

"**Add more questions**" allows you to create an informational question, a text question, a yes/no question or a multiple-choice question. You can add any type of question that your organization requires.

"**Use previous bapInterview questions**" will list all previous questions that you have created on this BAP framework. This greatly simplifies the creation of interviews as most of the time data collection/interviews have common questions.

Act

1. Choose an option works for you. The next page will show an example of adding more questions.

New question   ×

Type: *

┌───┐ ▼

Information Only

Yes/No Question

Text Question

Multiple Choice Question

                                                    [Yes] [No]

Insight

"**Information only**" allows you to place information with in the interview that requires no feedback from the person taking the interview. This allows for you to communicate information with in your reports and on to enhance the users experience of taking interview. Information only is a text-based field that has a limitation of 5000 characters. There is no validation available for the information only field.

"**Yes/no question**" is a yes/no question. Selecting this type of question will provide the user with a radio button to choose either yes or no as their answer. For validation, you can assign different weights to their response. For example, you may apply a 90% weight for yes answer and a 10% weight for no answer. The result of these weights will show on the final report as a red, yellow, or green light related to the question.

"**Text question**" is a text-based field that you can add any question you like and request a text-based answer. This is a validated field that allows you to add key phrases for the BAP AI to search for with in the user's response. This is a very powerful feature of BAP. If the user enters incorrect information, the user will receive a list of the key phrases associated with the answer providing them coaching on the type of information the interview originator is looking for.

"**Multiple-choice question**" allows you to enter an unlimited amount of multiple-choice answers. The user will respond by selecting one of the multiple-choice answers as a radio button. Multiple-choice questions, similar to the yes/no question allows for the weight allocation on the selected answer providing a visual indicator as to their response.

Act

1. **Choose the type of question** you would like to create for your interview, remember you can repeat this process as many times as you desire, and add an unlimited amount of questions.

2. Choose **yes** to continue to the next screen.

Previous bapInterview questions   ×

| | Add selected | | Search | | ▦▾ |

☐	**Title**	↕	**Type**
☐	Are you utilizing self-encrypting drives?		Yes/No Question
☐	Is this a desktop or a server?		Multiple Choice Question
☐	Please explain how your environment meets FIPS 140-2 requirements.		Text Question
☐	inf only		Information Only
☐	big text		Text Question
☐	4.2.3		Information Only
☐	Identification, authentication, and access control		Information Only
☐	How?		Text Question
☐	Does the system support federal user authentication via CAC/PIV credentials? [IA-2(12)]		Yes/No Question
☐	Interview		Text Question

Showing 1 to 10 of 146 rows   10 ▴   rows per page   ‹ **1** 2 3 4 5 ... 15 ›

Insight

Listed are previous questions that you've used on this framework for other interviews. BAP has collected all previous questions to streamline the build of new interviews.

If you choose the word "**Title**", all of your questions will be reorganized alphabetically and grouped by interview name and question type.

You may also search for a specific question using the **Search** box found on the upper right of the screen.

If you select the **small box** to the left of the word "Title" you will select all questions displayed on the current page. Illustrated on the screenshot above, at the lower left part of the screen, "**Showing 1 to 10 of 146 rows, 10 rows per page**" allows you to adjust the number of questions that appear on a page. If you are selecting the small box to the left of the word "title" and want to include all 146 questions in your next interview, you would need to adjust the number of rows appearing per page. You have the option to display up to 200 questions at one time per page. In this example, if you select a small box to the left of the word "title", and you have set up 200 rows per page, you will be able to select all 146 questions at one time.

When you select the "**Add selected**" button, it will add all questions that have a checkbox next to them (the checkbox will appear to the immediate left of the question, there are no boxes checked in the illustration).

Act

1. Choose the questions you would like to add to your interview.

2. Choose "**Add selected**" button to return to the interview creation screen.

Will the Cloud be used internally or as an IaaS platform?	▾

Add more options   Close box

4.2.3-Identification, authentication, and access control. Question #2

Does the system uniquely identify and authorize organizational users (or processes acting on behalf of organizational users) in a manner that cannot be repudiated and which sufficie	▾

How?

Documentation:

Interview:

Insight

A few key indicators for you on the screen. The drop-down box (to the far right of the question) indicates that you can add options related to the answers received by the user as they take the interview.

Illustrated on the screen we have selected the drop-down box associated with the question "**Will the cloud be used internally or as an IaaS platform**? This happens to be a multiple-choice question. Also illustrated it is the second question, "**Does the system uniquely identify…**", note the associated downward arrow. The second question is a yes/no question. If we had selected the down arrow, we would see a radio button for yes and another radio button for no, although because it is a yes/no question we cannot edit or add more options. We only add more options to multiple-choice questions.

Act

1. Choose "**Add more options**" to add more options to this multiple-choice question.

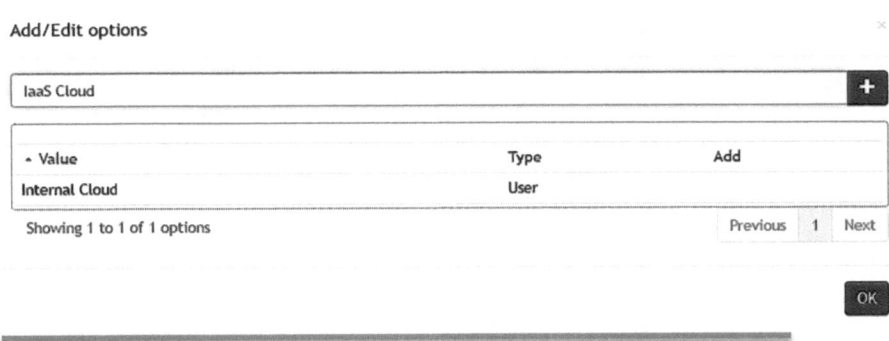

Insight

We can add or edit what will appear as radio buttons for the user to select as the correct answer for the multiple-choice question. Multiple-choice answers are effective, although should be limited if possible. Remember that multiple-choice answers can be validated and weighted, which we will discuss in a later chapter.

Act

1. Add the answer option. In the illustration above, we have added "IaaS cloud".

2. Choose the **"plus symbol"** (far right of the screen) to add the answer option to the list of options that will appear as an answer choice for the multiple-choice question.

Repeat steps 1 and 2 until you have added all of the multiple-choice answers for your multiple-choice question.

3. Choose **"OK"** when you have completed adding all of the multiple-choice answers for your multiple-choice question.

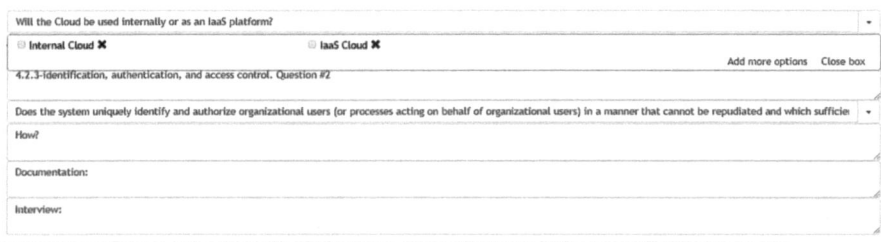

Insight

Illustrated are the multiple-choice answers that will be shown to the users they take the interview. To close the box illustrating the multiple-choice answers, choose the "**Close box**". If you would like to add additional options, choose "**Add more options**".

Act

1. When you have completed adding multiple-choice answers, choose the "**Next**" button in the lower right of the screen.

Fields to Validate:

☐	**Check All**			
☑	Does the system uniquely identify and authorize organizational users (or processes acting on behalf of organizational users) in a manner that cannot be repudiated and which sufficiently reduces the risk of impersonation? [IA-2, IA-4, IA-4(4)]		☑ Validate the field is not empty	
☑	How?		☑ Validate the field is not empty	
☑	Documentation:	☐ Validate the field is not empty	Edit key phrases to look for	Number: 0
☑	Interview:		☑ Validate the field is not empty	
☑	Will the Cloud be used internally or as an IaaS platform?	☐ Validate the field is not empty	Edit value weights to look for	

Insight

Now that we've established what the questions are going to be for the interview, we will need to add validation so that we can quickly and consistently validate the quality of the answers. The ability to validate questions is very helpful with understanding the integrity of the answers that have been collected.

On the far left of the screen are the check boxes indicating if you would like to validate the question or not. The default is to validate all questions so that they are not empty. This is the suggested minimum value for all interviews.

Listed just to the right of the checkbox is the question being asked in the interview, and to the far right is the checkbox indicating the type of validation that will occur to the question. The default is to "Validate that the field is not empty".

Note the question "documentation" in the illustration above. Notice that we have removed the checkbox from the "validate the field is not empty" option. To the far right of the question "documentation" are two fields: **"number"** and **"edit key phrases to look for"**.

"Number" (illustrated on the "documentation" question line above). The number indicates how many key phrases have been associated with the "documentation" question.

"Edit key phrases to look for" (illustrated on the "documentation" question line above). As you validate text found within answers provided by the user's, you will do this using key phrases. Key phrases are a common approach to understanding and validating information. Single key phrases, for example the words "to" and "the", etc. are not suggested key phrases. Key phrases we are looking for are more specific to the answer we may receive related to the question. For example: the question, different than illustrated above, may be, "how are you protecting data?". Key phrases for the question "how are you protecting data?" may include: cryptography, data at rest, self encrypting drives.

The fields to validate screen differs when you are working with technical versus non-technical interview questions. We will review the differences in another chapter of this book.

Act

1. Adjust the type of validation that will occur for every question. Remember this is a onetime activity, and can be used for multiple recipients.

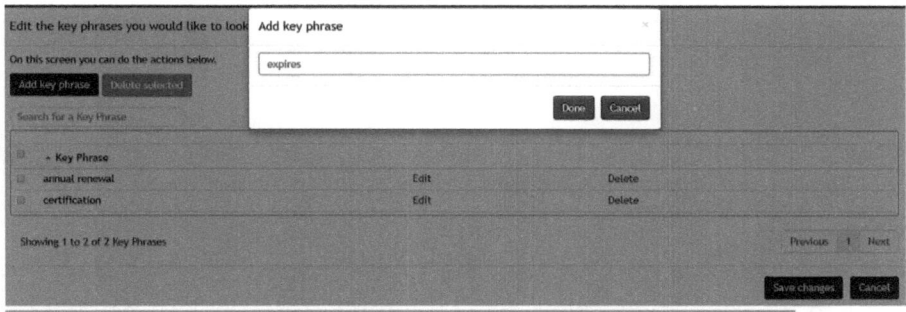

Insight

Key phrases allow you to look for information with in data collected to validate that the information aligns to your expectation for the question. The selection of key phrases is important, as you want to select key phrases that are unique. Key phrases are case-sensitive and will only search for the exact phrase entered on the screen. You can attach key phrases to any text-based field with in BAP interview. You can edit or delete key phrases or add key phrases at any time.

Key phrases are also provided to the user of the interview at immediate feedback and training. For example, you ask a question and are expecting specific information (key phrases) to be explained within the answer. Without the use of BAP and the automated and validated data collection model found within BAP interview, you may have to spend time collecting and clarifying answers received. BAP interview and BAP validate provides immediate feedback for users as to your expectation, ultimately providing a better answer.

Validation is very powerful with in certification activities, preventing organizations from receiving sizable fines associated with inaccurate information and answers to critical questions.

Act

1. **Add the appropriate key phrases** to the text-based questions with in your interview. Key phrases are not required, although suggested. If key phrases are not used, please consider at minimum validating to make sure the answer is not empty.

2. Choose **done** and **save changes**.

Edit the weights for the options you would like to look for

Each option may be given a weight as you need, in units of percentage. The only rule is that the sum of options weights must fulfill a total of 100%.

Value	Weight	
Internal Cloud	30	%
IaaS Cloud	70	%

Save changes   Cancel

Insight

For multiple-choice and yes/no questions you can add a weight to the answer received. This allows you to provide visual feedback as to the answer provided by the user. In the example illustrated above, the author of the interview, prefers users to select infrastructure as a service cloud (IaaS cloud) versus and internal cloud. This is an interesting feature that provides additional flexibility to the interview and data collection process.

Act

1. **Add the appropriate weights** to all multiple-choice and yes/no questions as desired.
2. Once the weights have been entered, choose **save changes**.

Fields to Validate:

	Check All			
☑	Does the system uniquely identify and authorize organizational users (or processes acting on behalf of organizational users) in a manner that cannot be repudiated and which sufficiently reduces the risk of impersonation? [IA-2, IA-4, IA-4(4)]		☑ Validate the field is not empty	
☑	How?		☑ Validate the field is not empty	
☑	Documentation:	☐ Validate the field is not empty	Edit key phrases to look for	Number: 3
☑	Interview:		☑ Validate the field is not empty	
☑	Will the Cloud be used internally or as an IaaS platform?	☐ Validate the field is not empty	Edit value weights to look for	

Insight

When you have completed the changes to all the questions, your questions may look like the illustration above.

Note on the "documentation" line that the number value is 3, indicating that three key phrases have been assigned to this question.

Note on the "will the cloud be used internally…" line, which is a multiple-choice question, that the "validate the field is not empty" checkbox is deselected indicating that weights have been added to this multiple-choice question.

Act

1. If everything looks good, choose next.

Refresh columns

1 - 4.2.3-identification, authentication, and access control. Question #2	5 - Documentation:
2 - Will the Cloud be used internally or as an IaaS platform?	6 - Interview:
3 - Does the system uniquely identify and authorize organizational users (or processes acting on behalf of organizational users) in a manner that cannot be repudiated and which sufficiently reduces the risk of impersonation? [IA-2, IA-4, IA-4(4)]	
4 - How?	

Insight

The order of the questions is illustrated on the screen. It is important to note that the order in which the screen illustrates, is the order in which the report will display the questions and answers.

Act

1. Using the left mouse button, select and hold down the left mouse button to drag a question to a new location. Release the mouse button to move the question.
2. Choose next to continue

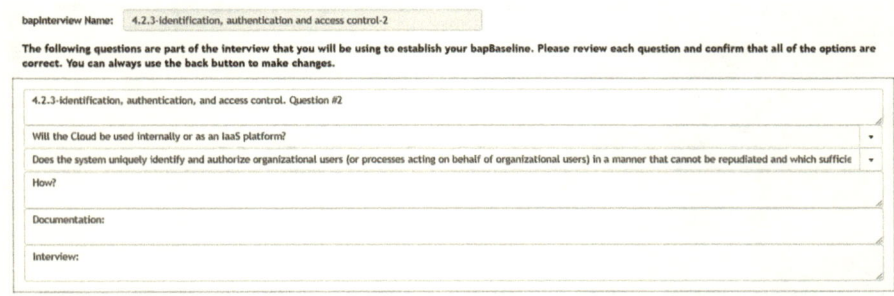

Insight

The preview screen is available for you to review and confirm that everything looks correct. If you are unsatisfied with a question, a response or the location of the question you can always go **"back"**, revise, and try again.

Act

1. Confirm everything looks correct
2. Choose **next** to continue to the package screen

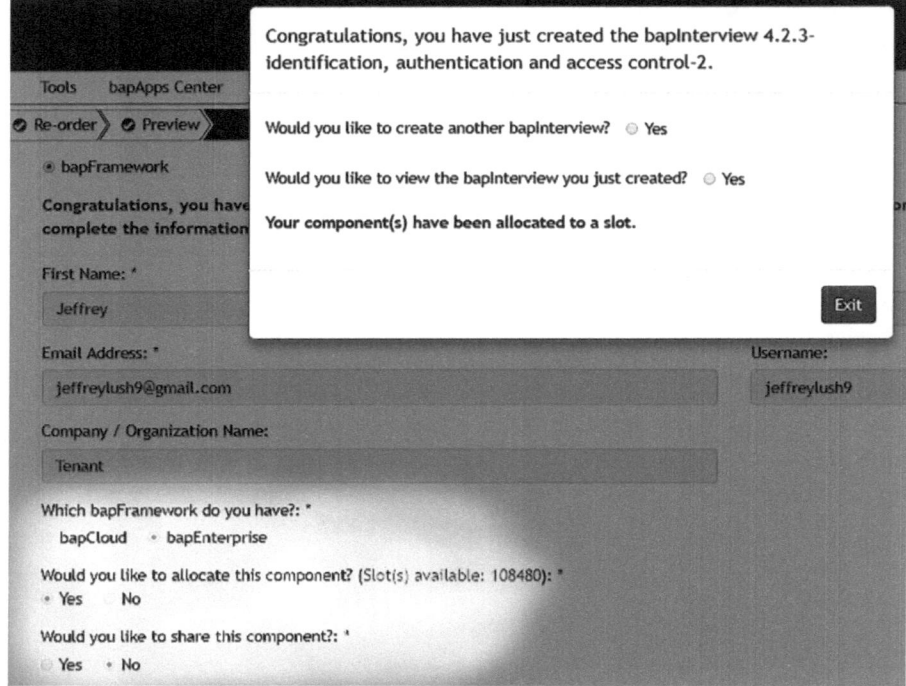

Insight

The package screen is very similar on every component. Your information will automatically populate, as will the choices have highlighted at the lower part of the screen illustrated above.

"**Which BAP framework do you have?**" BAP offers 2 different frameworks, BAP cloud in BAP enterprise. The default is BAP enterprise and is preselected for you.

BAP enterprise is a virtual appliance that can be hosted within a VMware hypervisor or a Microsoft hypervisor. Most of our customers use BAP enterprise.

BAP cloud is a software as a service solution offered by BAP with limited BAP services. If you are a BAP cloud tenant, you will have the option to save your work to your BAP cloud instance.

"**Would you like to allocate this component**" components are allocated to a slot or license on your system. Note that the slots available, illustrated above "slots available: 108480" indicate the number of slots available. The default is to select yes, although there may be instances where you are creating a component for another framework, or perhaps creating a component that will be used in the future. There is no limit to the number of components you can create.

"**Would you like to share this component?**" The default is no, although if you select yes you will be prompted to enter your email address or the email address of the individual you would like to share with. The component you have just created will be encrypted with a .BAP file extension and sent to the user. The files are very small and there are no restrictions for sharing components that you have authored with other BAP frameworks. If you purchased a component from the BAP marketplace, you will not be able to share that component unless the author has enabled sharing.

Once you have selected save, a pop-up screen will appear as illustrated above. You will receive two options.

"**Would you like to create another BAP interview?**" at which time BAP will bring you back to the BAP interview creation screen if you choose yes.

"**Would you like to preview the BAP interview you just created?** Will provide a preview of the interview you just created if you choose yes.

Also note if you have allocated a slot to be used with this component, it will indicate so at the bottom of the pop-up screen. Choose **exit** if neither of the options are appealing.

Act

1. To save the component, choose "**save**" in the lower right of the screen. Once you have successfully saved the component, the pop-up menu will appear as illustrated above.

2. Choose "**exit**" to return to the BAP opening screen.

Validate controls - bapInterview

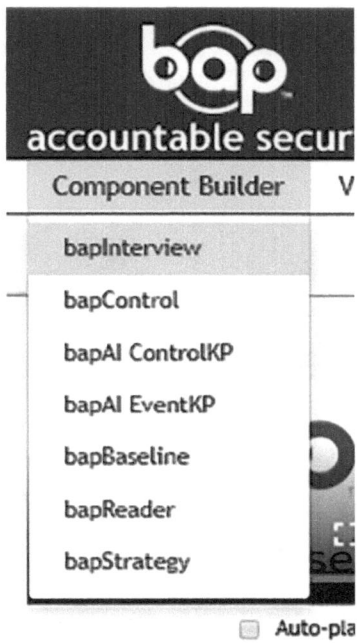

Insight

Just as you did in chapter 1, you will use the component builder to build the interview. The difference between chapter 1 and chapter 2 is that in chapter 1 you built an interview based on any question that came to your mind, whereas chapter 2 you will use either a baseline or a control to build an interview. As we walk through chapter 2, we will use a baseline to build a set of questions both technical and non-technical about that baseline.

This is a great option if you are building a system security plan, whereas you can collect information specific to a control and/or baseline, as well as custom questions, for example approving authority.

Act

1. Choose **component builder**, upper left of your screen
2. Choose **bapInterview**

Insight

In chapter 1 we chose "create a new bapInterview" to create an interview based on any question we desired to ask. In chapter 2 we will choose "**create bapInterview based on control or baseline**" which will present for us a baseline or control that we currently have installed within our bapFramework. If you do not have any controls or baselines loaded within your framework, this option will not work. Contact info@BAPsolution.com and ask for the initial setup of controls.

"**Edit a bapInterview**" allows you to edit an interview, which will follow the same screens as seen in chapter 1 and chapter 2. This book does not go into details around "Edit a bapInterview". If you choose "Edit a bapInterview" you will be able to choose an existing bapInterview and/or search for an interview you previously created or imported.

Act

1. Choose "**Create bapInterview based on control or baseline**" (far left of the screen).

○ bapBaseline ○ bapControl

bapInterview Name: * [_____] ⊞

required

Please select the questions you would like to ask the consumers in the interview to help them create a security baseline. You will "include" the que to include, or select the toggle to "No" to not include the question.

	No	How many servers are in the environment?	▾
	No	What hardware is in your environment?	▾
	No	System Owner	
	No	Company Name	
	No	What software is in your environment?	▾
	No	What operating system is in your environment?	▾
Include		SSP Development for HR System. Technical Controls	✕

[Add more questions] [Use previous bapInterview questions]

Insight

Just as in chapter 1, we have the option to create custom questions or select from previously used questions. At the top of the screen you will see two radio buttons "**bapBaseline**" and "**bapControl**".

"**bapBaseline**" provides all the controls related to this baseline to be used as questions. This is very helpful when creating an interview that is compliance oriented, making it very simple to ask all questions related to the baseline. In chapter 2, we will select "**bapBaseline**" for our discussion and insight.

"**bapControl**" provides a singular control to solicit information. In future chapters we will learn about **bapStrategy** which allows you to put multiple singular interviews together to create a unified interview made up of technical and non-technical interviews. Choosing "**bapControl**" allows you to develop only questions around specific controls, without having to create a baseline.

Act

1. Choose "**bapBaseline**"

Insight

We have selected **bapBaseline**, hence we see all baselines that are currently loaded within this bapFramework. You can preview the controls associated with this baseline by selecting the **preview** button. Remember your selection will add all the controls associated with this baseline as interview questions.

Act

1. **Choose a baseline** you would like to use to build your interview

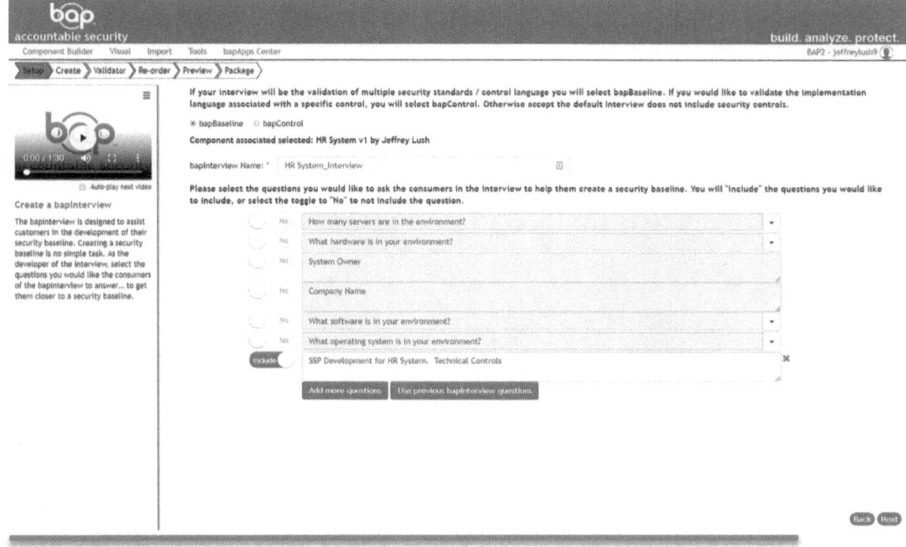

Insight

This is a result screen of your past two pages of actions. Note that the "**bapInterview name**" has been automatically added. On the previous screen we selected the "**HR System**" baseline. Note the BAP interview name is "**HR System_Interview**". The default interview name is the name of the baseline selected with a _Interview_ following name. You can modify this name if desired.

Act

1. You can add additional questions or choose previously used questions.
2. Choose **next** to continue

bapInterview Name: | HR System_Interview

The questions below doesn't have custom options.

SSP Development for HR System. Technical Controls

Insight

The "**Create**" screen is used to add options to multiple-choice questions. In this example, no multiple-choice questions are available, so no action is required. If a multiple-choice question was available, you would see an arrow at the far right of the question, indicating additional options were available.

Act

1. Choose **next** to continue

Check All					
☑ AC-6 Enh-1 LEAST PRIVILEGE | AUTH ACCESS TO SECURITY FUNCTIONS	Edit title question	🔍	Edit key phrases to look for	Number: 5
☑ SC-12 CRYPTO KEY ESTABLISHMENT & MGT	Edit title question	🔍	Edit key phrases to look for	Number: 10
☑ IA-4 a. IDENTIFIER MGT	Edit title question	🔍	Edit key phrases to look for	Number: 6
☑ AU-5 b. RESPONSE TO AUDIT PROCESSING FAILURES	Edit title question	🔍	Edit key phrases to look for	Number: 5
☑ AU-2 a. AUDIT EVENTS	Edit title question	🔍	Edit key phrases to look for	Number: 2
☑ SI-4 a-1 INFO SYS MONITORING	Edit title question	🔍	Edit key phrases to look for	Number: 5
☑ AC-3 ACCESS ENFORCEMENT	Edit title question	🔍	Edit key phrases to look for	Number: 2
☑ AU-6 a. AUDIT REVIEW, ANALYSIS, AND REPORTING	Edit title question	🔍	Edit key phrases to look for	Number: 5
☑ MP-4 a. MEDIA STORAGE	Edit title question	🔍	Edit key phrases to look for	Number: 5
☑ MP-2 MEDIA ACCESS	Edit title question	🔍	Edit key phrases to look for	Number: 3
☑ MP-5 a. MEDIA TRANSPORT	Edit title question	🔍	Edit key phrases to look for	Number: 5
☑ AC-5 a. SEPARATION OF DUTIES	Edit title question	🔍	Edit key phrases to look for	Number: 1
☑ MP-3 a. MEDIA MARKING	Edit title question	🔍	Edit key phrases to look for	Number: 6
☑ IA-2 Enh-8 ID AND AUTH (ORG USERS) | REPLAY RESIST	Edit title question	🔍	Edit key phrases to look for	Number: 5
☑ AC-19 a. ACCESS CONTROL FOR MOBILE DEVICES	Edit title question	🔍	Edit key phrases to look for	Number: 22
☑ AU-3 CONTENT OF AUDIT RECORDS	Edit title question	🔍	Edit key phrases to look for	Number: 8
☑ CM-7 Enh-5-a LEAST FUNCTIONALITY | WHITELISTING	Edit title question	🔍	Edit key phrases to look for	Number: 2
☑ CM-7 Enh-4-b LEAST FUNCTIONALITY | BLACKLISTING	Edit title question	🔍	Edit key phrases to look for	Number: 6

Insight

Because we have selected a baseline to build this interview upon we are now looking at all the controls associated with this baseline. Each control appears on a separate line or row. The first control is "AC-6…" and is on row 1.

The "**checkbox**" for row 1 is selected indicating that row 1 will be included as part of the validation associated with this interview. If validation is not desired, simply deselect the checkbox.

The name of the question for row 1 is "**AC-6…**" and can be changed by selecting "**Edit title question**" which we will show as the next screenshot available in this chapter. Often, customers edit the name of the control to make it easier for the user to understand the question.

The "**preview button**" allows you to preview the control language and implementation language associated with the control.

Notice in the far right of the screen for row 1 you will see "**Number: 5**". This number indicates the number of key phrases already associated with this control. You can edit the key phrases associated with this control by choosing "**Edit key phrases to look for**", which we will show as a screenshot later in this chapter.

Act

1. Decide if the control will be part of the interview questions and modify whether the control will be part of the interview by deselecting the checkbox far left of the row. The default is to include all rows.

2. Take the opportunity to modify the title of the question or the key phrases associated with the question

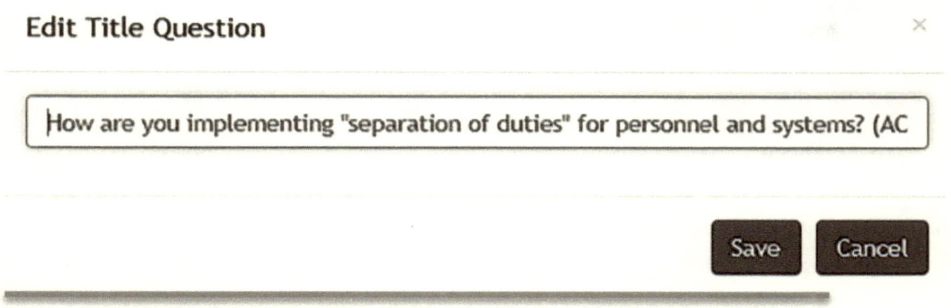

Edit Title Question   ×

How are you implementing "separation of duties" for personnel and systems? (AC

Save   Cancel

Insight

The above screenshot is looking at the AC-5 a interview question. Note that additional language is being added to make it easier for the user to provide the information we are seeking related to this control. Although not easily seen within the screenshot, note at the end of the question a reference to the control, typically added as (control name).

Act

1. Edit the titles of all questions.
2. Upon completing the edit of the title, choose **"save"** to save your work.
3. Choose "next" to continue

	▲ Key Phrase	Include
☐	access	CD ✖ - CL ✔ - IL ✔
☐	approved trust anchors	CD ✖ - CL ✔ - IL ✔
☐	certificates	CD ✖ - CL ✔ - IL ✔
☐	cryptographic keys	CD ✖ - CL ✔ - IL ✔
☐	cryptography	CD ✖ - CL ✔ - IL ✔
☐	destruction	CD ✖ - CL ✔ - IL ✔
☐	distribution	CD ✖ - CL ✔ - IL ✔
☐	key generation	CD ✖ - CL ✔ - IL ✔

Insight

Listed are all of the key phrases associated with this question. Remember key phrases are used as your validation, to confirm that the recipient of the interview is providing the information that you are looking for. For example, as the originator of the interview *I am interested in how they are generating keys.*

As the recipient of the interview I would include in my response, *"we have established a process to separate the roles and responsibilities associated with **key generation**..."*. Since the recipient includes the key phrase "**key generation**, in the implementation language the field is validated.

To perform actions to include edit and delete an existing key phrases, **choose the checkbox** to the left of the key phrase and then choose either "**Edit selected**" or "**Delete selected**".

Act

1. **Review, edit, add and delete** key phrases as desired

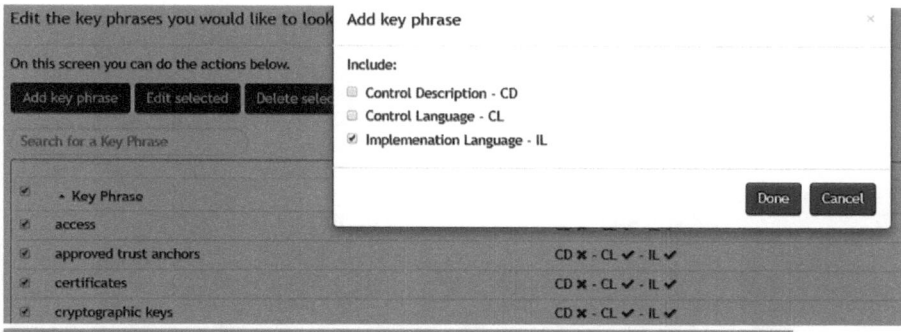

Insight

When an interview question is built upon a control, the key phrases associated with the control are automatically added as key phrases for the interview. The BAP AI will search for the key phrases entered by the recipient of the interview in the control language, control description or implementation language text boxes that are associated with the control.

If you choose to edit a single control, you will choose the checkbox to the left of that control and choose "**Edit selected**". You will then be prompted to change the name of the key phrase, as well as directions for the BAP AI search capability associated with this control. The BAP AI will only search the text boxes associated with the control that are selected from the screen above. The default for most customers is to only search the implementation language.

You can perform an edit of where the BAP AI will search on all the controls associated with an interview. To perform this action, choose the "**Checkbox to the left of the text key phrase**" at the top of the list of questions. By doing so, all of the checkboxes will be selected for each key phrase associated with this question. When you have selected "**Edit selected**" you will be able to change where the BAP AI will search. In the example above, we have chosen to only search for the key phrases found within the implementation language associated with each control.

Act

1. Adjust key phrases as desired.

Fields to Validate:

☐	**Check All**				
☑	AC-6 Enh-1 LEAST PRIVILEGE | AUTH ACCESS TO SECURITY FUNCTIONS	Edit title question	🔍	Edit key phrases to look for	Number: 5
☑	SC-12 CRYPTO KEY ESTABLISHMENT & MGT	Edit title question	🔍	Edit key phrases to look for	Number: 10
☑	IA-4 a. IDENTIFIER MGT	Edit title question	🔍	Edit key phrases to look for	Number: 6
☑	AU-5 b. RESPONSE TO AUDIT PROCESSING FAILURES	Edit title question	🔍	Edit key phrases to look for	Number: 5
☑	AU-2 a. AUDIT EVENTS	Edit title question	🔍	Edit key phrases to look for	Number: 2
☑	SI-4 a-1 INFO SYS MONITORING	Edit title question	🔍	Edit key phrases to look for	Number: 5
☑	AC-3 ACCESS ENFORCEMENT	Edit title question	🔍	Edit key phrases to look for	Number: 2
☑	AU-6 a. AUDIT REVIEW, ANALYSIS, AND REPORTING	Edit title question	🔍	Edit key phrases to look for	Number: 5
☑	What is your strategy for media storage? (MP-4 a)	Edit title question	🔍	Edit key phrases to look for	Number: 5
☑	MP-2 MEDIA ACCESS	Edit title question	🔍	Edit key phrases to look for	Number: 5
☑	MP-5 a. MEDIA TRANSPORT	Edit title question	🔍	Edit key phrases to look for	Number: 3
☑	How are you implementing "separation of duties" for personnel and systems? (AC-5 a.)	Edit title question	🔍	Edit key phrases to look for	Number: 1
☑	MP-3 a. MEDIA MARKING	Edit title question	🔍	Edit key phrases to look for	Number: 6
☑	IA-2 Enh-8 ID AND AUTH (ORG USERS) | REPLAY RESIST	Edit title question	🔍	Edit key phrases to look for	Number: 5
☑	AC-19 a. ACCESS CONTROL FOR MOBILE DEVICES	Edit title question	🔍	Edit key phrases to look for	Number: 22
☑	AU-3 CONTENT OF AUDIT RECORDS	Edit title question	🔍	Edit key phrases to look for	Number: 8
☑	CM-7 Enh-5-a LEAST FUNCTIONALITY | WHITELISTING	Edit title question	🔍	Edit key phrases to look for	Number: 2
☑	CM-7 Enh-4-b LEAST FUNCTIONALITY | BLACKLISTING	Edit title question	🔍	Edit key phrases to look for	Number: 6

Insight

This is a result screen of the actions that you have taken on the past couple of screens. Note rows 9 and 12 we have modified the questions.

Act

1. Choose **next** to proceed

Refresh columns

1 - SSP Development for HR System. Technical Controls

2 - How are you implementing "separation of duties" for personnel and systems? (AC-5 a.)

3 - What is your strategy for media storage? (MP-4 a)

4 - AC-6 Enh-1 LEAST PRIVILEGE | AUTH ACCESS TO SECURITY FUNCTIONS

5 - SC-12 CRYPTO KEY ESTABLISHMENT & MGT

6 - IA-4 a. IDENTIFIER MGT

7 - AU-5 b. RESPONSE TO AUDIT PROCESSING FAILURES

8 - AU-2 a. AUDIT EVENTS

9 - SI-4 a-1 INFO SYS MONITORING

10 - AC-3 ACCESS ENFORCEMENT

11 - AU-6 a. AUDIT REVIEW, ANALYSIS, AND REPORTING

12 - MP-2 MEDIA ACCESS

13 - MP-5 a. MEDIA TRANSPORT

14 - MP-3 a. MEDIA MARKING

15 - IA-2 Enh-8 ID AND AUTH (ORG USERS) | REPLAY RESIST

16 - AC-19 a. ACCESS CONTROL FOR MOBILE DEVICES

17 - AU-3 CONTENT OF AUDIT RECORDS

18 - CM-7 Enh-5-a LEAST FUNCTIONALITY | WHITELISTING

19 - CM-7 Enh-4-b LEAST FUNCTIONALITY | BLACKLISTING

Insight

The order of the questions is illustrated on the screen. It is important to note that the order in which the screen illustrates, is the order in which the report will display the questions and answers.

Act

1. Using the left mouse button, select and hold down the left mouse button to drag a question to a new location. Release the mouse button to move the question.

2. Choose **next** to continue

bapInterview Name: HR System_Interview

The following questions are part of the interview that you will be using to establish your bapBaseline. Please review each question and confirm that all of the options are correct. You can always use the back button to make changes.

SSP Development for HR System. Technical Controls
How are you implementing "separation of duties" for personnel and systems? (AC-5 a.)
What is your strategy for media storage? (MP-4 a)
AC-6 Enh-1 LEAST PRIVILEGE | AUTH ACCESS TO SECURITY FUNCTIONS
SC-12 CRYPTO KEY ESTABLISHMENT & MGT
IA-4 a. IDENTIFIER MGT
AU-5 b. RESPONSE TO AUDIT PROCESSING FAILURES
AU-2 a. AUDIT EVENTS
SI-4 a-1 INFO SYS MONITORING
AC-3 ACCESS ENFORCEMENT
AU-6 a. AUDIT REVIEW, ANALYSIS, AND REPORTING
MP-2 MEDIA ACCESS
MP-5 a. MEDIA TRANSPORT
MP-3 a. MEDIA MARKING
IA-2 Enh-8 ID AND AUTH (ORG USERS) | REPLAY RESIST
AC-19 a. ACCESS CONTROL FOR MOBILE DEVICES
AU-3 CONTENT OF AUDIT RECORDS
CM-7 Enh-5-a LEAST FUNCTIONALITY | WHITELISTING
CM-7 Enh-4-b LEAST FUNCTIONALITY | BLACKLISTING

Insight

The preview screen is available for you to review and confirm that everything looks correct. If you are unsatisfied with a question, a response or the location of the question you can always go "**back**", revise, and try again.

Act

1. Confirm everything looks correct
2. Choose **next** to continue to the package screen

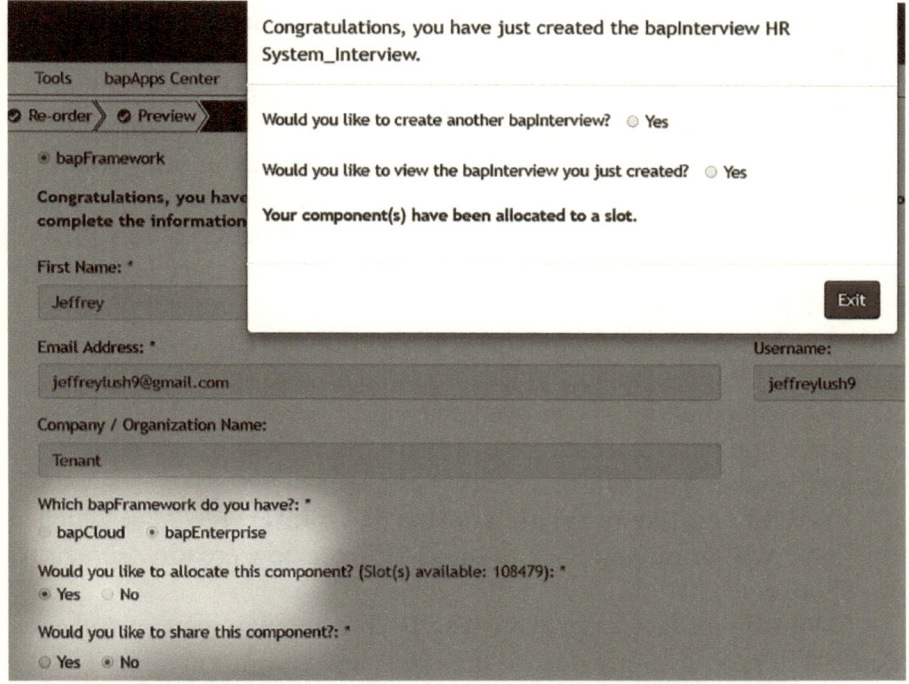

Insight

The package screen is very similar on every component. Your information will automatically populate, as will the choices have highlighted at the lower part of the screen illustrated above.

"**Which BAP framework do you have?**" BAP offers 2 different frameworks, BAP cloud in BAP enterprise. The default is BAP enterprise and is preselected for you.

BAP enterprise is a virtual appliance that can be hosted within a VMware hypervisor or a Microsoft hypervisor. Most of our customers use BAP enterprise.

BAP cloud is a software as a service solution offered by BAP with limited BAP services. If you are a BAP cloud tenant, you will have the option to save your work to your BAP cloud instance.

"**Would you like to allocate this component**" components are allocated to a slot or license on your system. Note that the slots available, illustrated above "slots available: 108479" indicate the number of slots available. The default is to select yes, although there may be instances where you are creating a component for another framework, or perhaps creating a component that will be used in the future. There is no limit to the number of components you can create.

"Would you like to share this component?" The default is no, although if you select yes you will be prompted to enter your email address or the email address of the individual you would like to share with. The component you have just created will be encrypted with a .BAP file extension and sent to the user. The files are very small and there are no restrictions for sharing components that you have authored with other BAP frameworks. If you purchased a component from the BAP marketplace, you will not be able to share that component unless the author has enabled sharing.

Once you have selected save, a pop-up screen will appear as illustrated above. You will receive two options.

"Would you like to create another BAP interview?" at which time BAP will bring you back to the BAP interview creation screen if you choose yes.

"Would you like to preview the BAP interview you just created? Will provide a preview of the interview you just created if you choose yes.

Also note if you have allocated a slot to be used with this component, it will indicate so at the bottom of the pop-up screen. Choose **exit** if neither of the options are appealing.

Act

1. To save the component, choose **"save"** in the lower right of the screen. Once you have successfully saved the component, the pop-up menu will appear as illustrated above.

2. Choose **"exit"** to return to the BAP opening screen.

Chapter three

Sharing my Interview

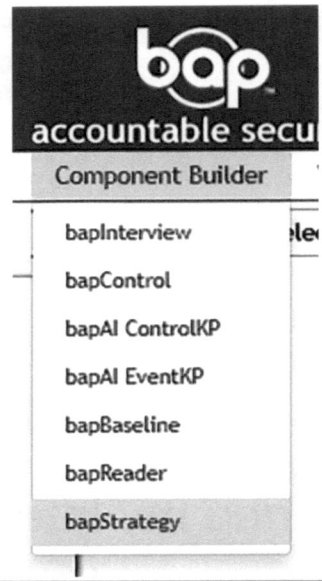

Insight

bapStrategy is the ability to combine multiple interviews into a single file and reporting mechanism. For example, you're creating a system security plan built upon a collection of controls for your HR system. In addition to the information related to the controls for the HR system, you will also be collecting site information, names of owners of specific tasks, and perhaps the approving authority information.

The collection of technical and non-technical interview questions requires an application that can present both as a single interview process, which is bapStrategy.

Act

1. Choose "**Component builder**" (in the upper left of your screen)
2. Choose "**bapStrategy**"

Create a new
bapStrategy

Edit a
bapStrategy

Insight

"**Create a new bapStrategy**" allows you to create a new BAP strategy file built upon interviews that you have already completed.

"**Edit a bapStrategy**" allows you to edit an existing BAP strategy file that you have created or imported. The only difference when "editing" a bapStrategy is that you will be presented with a list, search enabled, that will allow you to find the BAP strategy you wish to edit. You will be able to either choose the file and begin editing the information or choose the preview button to preview the strategy file. You will then be presented with screens that look very similar to creating a new BAP strategy.

Act

1. For this book, choose "**Create a new bapStrategy**"

bapStrategy Name: *

System Security Plan (SSP)

Description: *

Development of the organizations SSP for compliance activities

Insight

The example we will follow in this chapter will be based upon us creating a new bapStrategy.

Remember when entering a name if you are going to distribute this file for others to complete, you will want to name that is recognizable by those you are distributing to.

If you are creating the bapStrategy to be used as a template, you may want to consider giving the template a generic name, and then customizing the name to the copied version. For example, the bapStrategy file is named "System security plan (SSP)" as a generic name as this file will be used as a template for multiple sites. The "System security plan (SSP)" strategy will be cloned for other sites, like Tucson, and received the name "*System security plan (SSP)-Tucson*". We will discuss cloning of components in a later chapter.

Act

1. **Enter a name** of your bapStrategy.
2. Enter a **description** of your bapStrategy.

Select a baseline for associate with bapStrategy: ☐ Do not apply

bapBaseline Associated:

Search for a bapBaseline

◦ bapBaseline Name	Status		Preview
HR System v1 by Jeffrey Lush	Allocated	Select	🔍

Showing 1 to 1 of 1 bapBaselines

Insight

This is a two-step process. We will associate a baseline-based interview (for the HR system) with non-technical interviews.

"Select a baseline for associate with bapStrategy". If you select the checkbox the baseline will not be required, and you can move directly to the non-technical interview questions. In this example, we will select the "HR system" baseline

Choose the **"Preview"** button to review the contents of the baseline.

Act

1. Choose the **"select"** text to include the baseline.

Description:

Development of the organizations SSP for compliance activities

bapBaseline Associated:

HR System v1 by Jeffrey Lush

bapValidates Associated with bapBaseline:

Search for a bapValidate

▲ bapValidate name
HR System_Interview v1 by Jeffrey Lush

Showing 1 to 1 of 1 bapValidates

Components Associated:

Non Control bapValidate

Search for a Non Control bapValid

▲ Non Control bapValidate name
4.2.3 identification, authentication, and access control-1 v1 by Jeffrey Lush
4.2.3-identification, authentication and access control-2 v2 by Jeffrey Lush

Insight

The **"preview"** screen allows you to see the name of the baseline selected, which in this case is *"HR System_Interview"*, as well as the non-control based interview questions that have been included, as illustrated above *"4.2.3 identification, authentication..."*. The top of the screen also shows the **"description"** and the **associated baseline** name, as illustrated *"HR System_Interview"*.

Act

1. **Review and confirm** that the correct interviews are grouped together on the screen. If they are not, choose the **"back"** button to make changes.
2. If everything looks okay, choose the **"next"** button to proceed.

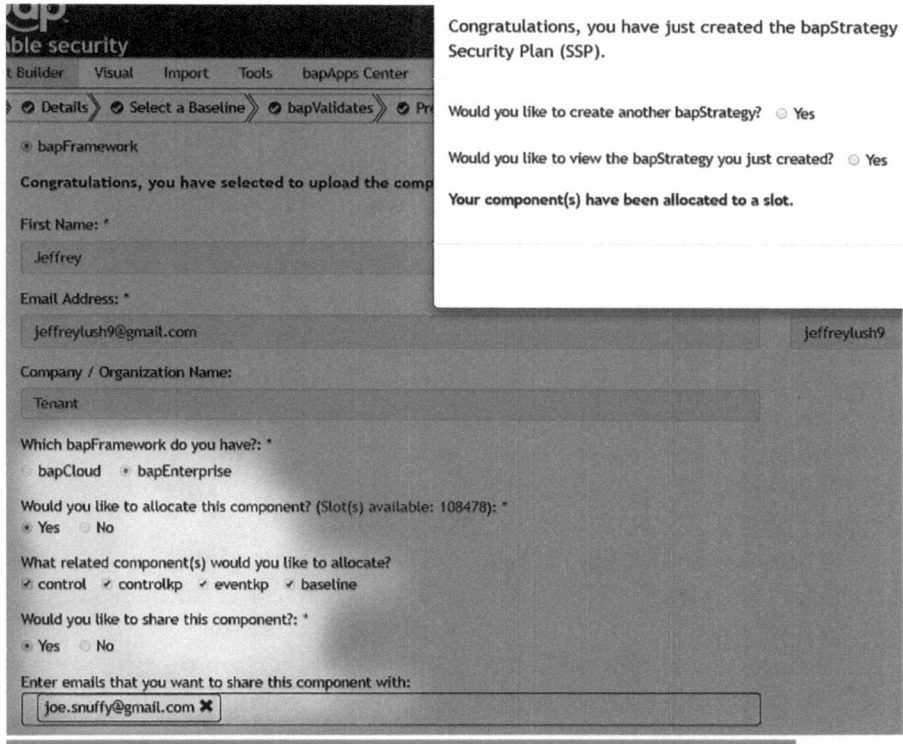

Insight

The package screen is very similar on every component. Your information will automatically populate, as will the choices have highlighted at the lower part of the screen illustrated above.

"**Which BAP framework do you have?**" BAP offers 2 different frameworks, BAP cloud in BAP enterprise. The default is BAP enterprise and is preselected for you.

BAP enterprise is a virtual appliance that can be hosted within a VMware hypervisor or a Microsoft hypervisor. Most of our customers use BAP enterprise.

BAP cloud is a software as a service solution offered by BAP with limited BAP services. If you are a BAP cloud tenant, you will have the option to save your work to your BAP cloud instance.

"**Would you like to allocate this component**" components are allocated to a slot or license on your system. Note that the slots available, illustrated above "slots available: 108478" indicate the number of slots available. The default is to select yes, although there may be instances where you are creating a component for another framework, or perhaps creating a component that will be used in the future. There is no limit to the number of components you can create.

"**Would you like to share this component?**" The default is no, although if you select yes you will be prompted to enter your email address or the email address of the individual you would like to share with. The component you have just created will be encrypted with a .BAP file extension and sent to the user. The files are very small and there are no restrictions for sharing components that you have authored with other BAP frameworks. If you purchased a component from the BAP marketplace, you will not be able to share that component unless the author has enabled sharing.

Once you have selected save, a pop-up screen will appear as illustrated above. You will receive two options.

"**Would you like to create another BAP interview?**" at which time BAP will bring you back to the BAP interview creation screen if you choose yes.

"**Would you like to preview the BAP interview you just created?** Will provide a preview of the interview you just created if you choose yes.

Also note if you have allocated a slot to be used with this component, it will indicate so at the bottom of the pop-up screen. Choose **exit** if neither of the options are appealing.

Act

1. To save the component, choose "**save**" in the lower right of the screen. Once you have successfully saved the component, the pop-up menu will appear as illustrated above.

2. Choose "**exit**" to return to the BAP opening screen.

Clone your bapStrategy

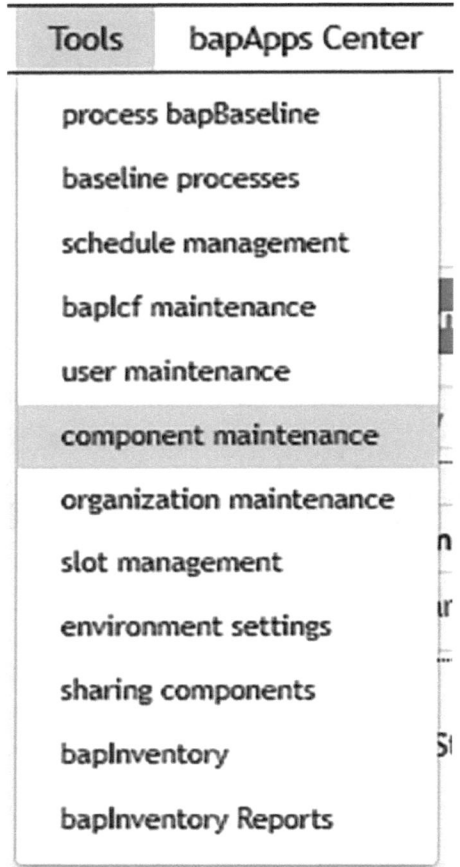

Insight

So far, chapters 1 through 3 have taken you through the process as the originator of the interview on how to create the interview and add validation for that interview. The chronological order of chapter 4 and chapter 5 may differ dependent upon your objectives.

BAP strategy is the collection of multiple interviews, both technical and non-technical to create a single interview for your recipient(s). You may want to consider using the initial creation of your BAP strategy as a "template". An example of the need to clone an interview may be an interview that is performed repeatedly with different recipients, perhaps you are developing multiple RARs (risk assessment reports) that require you to ask the same questions to multiple sites. With this example, you may create a BAP strategy called "RAR-Tucson" when perform the risk assessment at the Tucson facility. When you perform the same RAR interview in Seattle, you would return and clone your strategy and rename it to "RAR-Seattle".

If the strategy file is for a single user and will never be repeated, you could export the file and save it to be reloaded at a future date, clone the strategy file and name it "strategy file name-backup", or using VM tools with in BAP create a backup upon finishing your strategy so that a restore is possible in the future.

In this chapter, we will select to clone the strategy file so that it can be used for site-specific interviews.

Act

1. Choose **component builder** (upper left of your screen)
2. Choose **component maintenance** if you desire to clone the component.

bapControl	bapAI ControlKP	bapAI EventKP	bapBaseline	bapInterview	bapReader	bapStrategy

Remove selected component(s)

Search for a bapStrategy

• bapStrategy Name	Author	Last Modified	Status	Preview	Clone
System Security Plan (SSP) v1 by Jeffrey Lush	Jeffrey Lush	10/19/2018 15:38	Enabled		

Insight

Component maintenance is broken down by the components found within the BAP framework. Starting at the far left of your screen, and the upper left side, the following components can have maintenance completed: bapControl, bapAI ControlKP, bapAI EventKP, bapBaseline, bapInterview, bapReader, and bapStrategy.

To perform action to a bapStrategy, you must **select the checkbox** in the far left of the row with the strategy name. In the illustrated example above, there is only one bapStrategy.

Using the **search button** will allow you to search for a file.

The "preview" button will allow you to preview all of the sub-components associated with the component.

The "lock symbol" allows you to allocate and de-allocate the component. When a component is allocated it consumes a licensing slot.

Select the checkbox to the left of the component, then select **"Remove selected component(s)"** to remove the selected component.

Act

1. Select the **checkbox to the left of** " System Security Plan (SSP).
2. **"Clone"** button.

Clone component   ×

Please, type the name of the new cloned component

SSP for Tucson Office

[Save] [Cancel]

Insight

When cloning a component, you will copy all variables associated with that component. In this example we are cloning a sample "SSP" to become the SSP for the Tucson office.

Act

1. **Enter a name** for the component, as illustrated "*SSP for Tucson office*" is the name selected for this exercise. Please choose a name that works for your organization and the purpose of the cloned component.
2. Choose the "**save**" button to save your efforts.

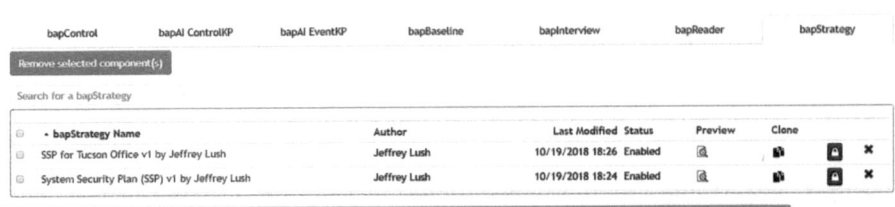

Insight

Illustrated in the example is the cloned result from cloning the "System Security Plan (SSP) to "SSP for Tucson Office"

Act

1. Confirm the information is correct.

Export your bapStrategy

bapApps Center
import bapStrategy
export bapStrategy
import bapValidate
export bapValidate
bapValidate
my bapCheck
org bapCheck
bapReader
bapReader Processes
demo ControlKP
demo EventKP
demo QuickCheck
wizard bapStrategy
bapRemediate
bapRemediate Report

Insight

When working with bapStrategy files there is a specific way to import and export the bapStrategy file. All other components found within the bapFramework can be shared through the tools menu option/share component. Although, with the bapStrategy file we are exporting a series of questions, soliciting feedback from the recipients, and processing all the information together for results. Because of this complexity, bapStrategy and bapInterview have isolated import and export functionality.

BAP provides two levels of service related to automated and validated data collection. Our first, covered extensively within this book, is found within the bapEnterprise virtual appliance. All the screens with in this book speak to bapEnterprise virtual appliance. For data collection that is sensitive by nature, bapEnterprise virtual appliance can be installed anywhere within your organization from a highly secure area to a moderately secure area. We strongly suggest for data collection efforts that are sensitive in the types of data you are collecting, bapEnterprise virtual appliance is the suggested application.

For automated and validated data collection that does not require as much stringent security, we have bapCloud. bapCloud is a multitenant hosted cloud service. Just like all hosted cloud services, there is a level of risk associated with placing data in a public forum. Please review the bapPress book on "Automated and Validated Data Collection via the Cloud" for additional information.

Act

1. Choose **bapApps Center** (the far upper right of the screen).
2. Choose **Export bapStrategy**.

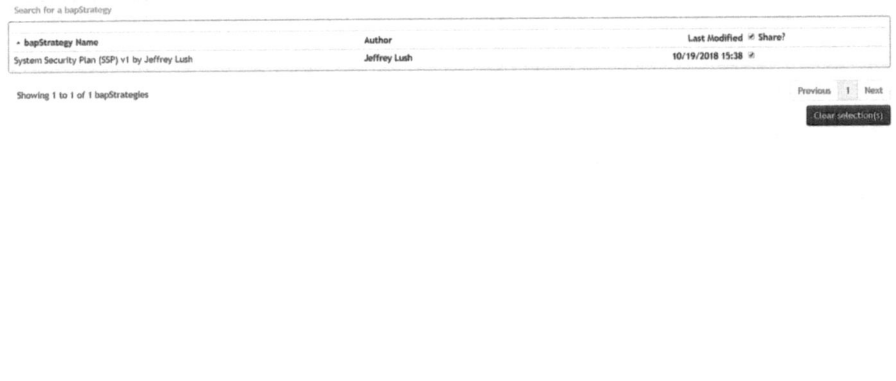

Insight

This is a two-step process. First we select the bapStrategy file(s) we would like to share. We can choose multiple files to share, although only one is illustrated on the screen above, but be mindful that if you select to share multiple strategy files they will be packaged together. If the Strategy/Interviews are going to the same recipient, great, otherwise you may want to consider sharing them individually.

Act

1. Choose the **checkbox** of the row associated with the component you would like to share.
2. Choose "**apply**" on the lower right side of the screen

Here you can see all components which will be packaged to

Search for a bapStrategy

▲ **Shared Component Name**

System Security Plan (SSP) v1 by Jeffrey Lush

Showing 1 to 1 of 1 bapStrategies

How do you want to share this package of components?

[Download] [Send by email] [Go Back]

Insight

"**Download**" will allow you to download the encrypted and compressed file with the components you have chosen to share. You can then email the file to other recipients and bapFrameworks. It's important to note that components can be shared freely between frameworks, although will require a license/slot to be allocated within any bapFramework.

"**Send by email**" will prompt BAP to send your component via email. This option is set up with in the environmental settings found within BAP (tools, environment settings). If you do not have your environmental settings set up correctly, the send by email will not function properly.

"**Go back**" allows you to abort the share and start over. The example we will use with in this book will illustrate how to download the component and then rename that component for distribution and/or storage.

Act

1. Choose "**download**"

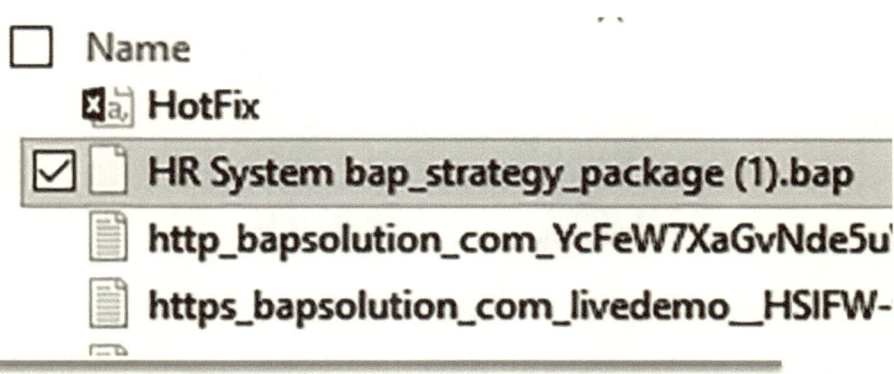

Insight

Rename the file to be personal to your environment. The default is "bap_strategy_package.bap". As illustrated above personalize the file.

Act

1. Rename the file as appropriate.

Import bapStrategy

bapApps Center

import bapStrategy

export bapStrategy

import bapValidate

export bapValidate

bapValidate

my bapCheck

org bapCheck

bapReader

bapReader Processes

demo ControlKP

demo EventKP

demo QuickCheck

wizard bapStrategy

bapRemediate

bapRemediate Report

Insight

When working with bapStrategy files there is a specific way to import and export the bapStrategy file. All other components found within the bapFramework can be shared through the tool menu option/share component. Although, with the bapStrategy file we are exporting a series of questions, soliciting feedback from the recipients, and processing all the information together for results. Because of this complexity, bapStrategy and bapInterview have isolated import and export functionality.

BAP provides two levels of service related to automated and validated data collection. Our first, covered extensively within this book, is found within the bapEnterprise virtual appliance. All the screens with in this book speak to bapEnterprise virtual appliance. For data collection that is sensitive by nature, bapEnterprise virtual appliance can be installed anywhere within your organization from a highly secure area to a moderately secure area. We strongly suggest for data collection efforts that are sensitive in the types of data you are collecting, bapEnterprise virtual appliance is the suggested application.

For automated and validated data collection that does not require as much stringent security, we have bapCloud. bapCloud is a multitenant hosted cloud service. Just like all hosted cloud services, there is a level of risk associated with placing data in a public forum. Please review the bapPress book on "Automated and Validated Data Collection via the Cloud" for additional information.

Act

1. Choose **bapApps Center** (the far upper right of the screen).
2. Choose **Import bapStrategy**.

Confirm Import   ×

Dependent upon the number and type of components, the import of the components may take several minutes. BAP will display a green progress box to let you know that we are working on the import. Some imports can take as long as 5 minutes for thousands of components. Thank you for your patience.

[Continue]   [Cancel]

Insight

Dependent upon the size of the component, it may take a few minutes to download the components.

Act

1. Choose "**continue**"

Import bapStrategy Clear file(s)

• Name	Component Type	Author	Version	Validated?	Imported?	Allocated?
4.2.3 identification, authentication, and access control-1	bapValidate	Jeffrey Lush	1	✔	✔	✔
4.2.3-identification, authentication and access control-2	bapValidate	Jeffrey Lush	2	✔	✔	✔
4.2.3-identification, authentication, and access control-4	bapValidate	Jeffrey Lush	1	✔	✔	✔
4.2.3-identification, authentication, and access control-5	bapValidate	Jeffrey Lush	1	✔	✔	✔
4.2.3-identification, authentication, and access control-6	bapValidate	Jeffrey Lush	1	✔	✔	✔
4.2.3-identification, authentication, and access control-7	bapValidate	Jeffrey Lush	1	✔	✔	✔
4.2.3-identification, authentication, and access control-8	bapValidate	Jeffrey Lush	1	✔	✔	✔
4.2.3-identification, authentication, and access control-9	bapValidate	Jeffrey Lush	1	✔	✔	✔
4.2.4-audit, alerting, malware, and incident response-1	bapValidate	Jeffrey Lush	1	✔	✔	✔
4.2.4-audit, alerting, malware, and incident response-2	bapValidate	Jeffrey Lush	1	✔	✔	✔

Showing 1 to 10 of 67 components

Previous 1 2 3 4 5 6 7 Next

Save bapStrategy

Insight

Importing a component is relatively simple.

"**Import bapStrategy**" is selected prior to finding the file that will be imported. Remember the file must have a BAP extension. Upon import, all the controls, the component type and the author will be illustrated. You will also notice the version number and a row of checkmarks down the "**Validated?**" column.

"**Imported**" verifies that the component was imported into the existing bapFramework.

"**Allocated**" verifies that a slot/license has been allocated for the component to work properly with in the bapFramework. Allocation is the default standard, if for some reason you choose not to allocate a component, you can go to tools, slot management to deallocate the component.

Act

1. Choose the "**import bapStrategy**"
2. Choose the file with the BAP extension that will be imported (.BAP)
3. Choose "**save bapStrategy**"
4. Choose "**next**" when three columns of checkboxes appear. Remember this may take a few minutes.

Take the bapInterview(s)

bapApps Center
import bapStrategy
export bapStrategy
import bapValidate
export bapValidate
bapValidate
my bapCheck
org bapCheck
bapReader
bapReader Processes
demo ControlKP
demo EventKP
demo QuickCheck
wizard bapStrategy
bapRemediate
bapRemediate Report

Insight

The recipient of the interview will go to the wizard for bapStrategy to complete the interview. Although illustrated above are multiple options, in many cases the user rights needed to be a recipient of an interview will dramatically reduce the number of menus and options available to the recipient. The drop-down menu that we are seeing in this example belongs to a site administrator.

It is important to note that the interview must be imported prior to the recipient using the interview. There are two ways to import an interview: "import BAP strategy" or "import BAP validate"

Act

1. Choose "**bapApps Center**"
2. Choose "**wizard bapStrategy**"

• bapStrategy Name	Last Modified	Status
System Security Plan (SSP) v1 by Jeffrey Lush	10/19/2018 17:07	Pending

Showing 1 to 1 of 1 bapStrategies   Previous 1 Next

Insight

The import of any component can take a few minutes. It is important to note under the status column "**pending**". Continue to refresh the page to find the status.

Act

1. Choose "**refresh**" as needed to update status

Insight

The "**status**" column (far right associated with each row/interview) provides a status as to the progress being made on the interview. The design of the user interface is to provide immediate feedback, especially for interviews that could have hundreds of questions.

"**Not started**" indicates that the interview has not been opened or started.

"**Started**" indicates that the interview has been started although the answers are not complete and accepted. Accepting your answers comes through the valuation screen that we will see later in this chapter.

"**Completed**" indicates the interview has been accepted and completed. Once completed the interview cannot be modified.

Act

1. Choose an interview and begin completing the answers.

> ⊘ Import bapStrategy ⟩⟩ ⊘ Choose a bapInterview ⟩ Questions ⟩ Controls ⟩ Review ⟩ Evaluation ⟩

Please, answer the following questions:

4.2.3-identification, authentication, and access control. Question #1

Does the system support federal user authentication via CAC/PIV credentials? [IA-2(12)]

⦿ Yes ○ No

How?

We have established an LDAP server in addition to our AD Server. They are both clustered for high availability.

Documentation:

Yes. We have detailed documentation at \FPC1\FISMACert\

Interview:

During the interview, we validated that the LDAP and AD servers are functional.

We recommend that the site uses BAP to add continuous monitoring to establish the control strength in real-time.

Insight

Notice the menu bar that extends horizontally across top of the screen and the checkmarks as those menu sections are visited. At any time, you can return to one of the horizontal menus. As illustrated above, we are currently on the "**questions**" horizontal menu.

Completion of the questions is very straightforward. Click on the radio buttons, or input information into the boxes.

Note the text "4.to.3-identification, authentication…". This text is an information field when setting up the interview.

Act

1. **Complete all the information** asked on the screen
2. Choose "**next**" when ready.

You have completed the 4.2.3 identification, authentication, and access control-1 interview, congratulations.

4.2.3-identification, authentication, and access control. Question #1
Does the system support federal user authentication via CAC/PIV credentials? [IA-2(12)]
Yes

Field Name	Score
Does the system support federal user authentication via CAC/PIV credentials? [IA-2(12)]	100.00% ●

How?
We have established an LDAP server in addition to our AD Server. They are both clustered for high availability.

Field Name	Score
How?	100.00% ●

Documentation:
Yes. We have detailed documentation at \FPC1\FISMACert\

Field Name	Score
Documentation:	100.00% ●

Interview:
During the interview, we validated that the LDAP and AD servers are functional. We recommend that the site uses BAP to add continuous monitoring to establish the control strength in real-time.

Field Name	Score
Interview:	100.00% ●

☐ Simplified Report (Download Text) (Download CSV) (Send to Mobile) (Open Report) (Send Report) (Evaluation)

Insight

This is the on-screen validation of the interview completed. At the very top of the screen "**you have completed the 4.2.3…**" is the name of the interview. This is the name given at the inception of the interview by the author.

On the second line which starts with "**4.to.3-identification,…**", is an informational field that was established during the development of the interview.

The **Yes/No question** is found on the third line, with the answer "**Yes**" on the fourth line.

The next four sections, all separated by a box called "field name" are the questions, answers and validation scores.

The **validation scores** appear on the right margin of the screen. Remember the validation scores are built upon the validation criteria created during the authoring of the interview.

At the bottom of the screen, starting from the left to the right, the checkbox "**simplified report**" will show on the screen only the questions and answers. This makes it easier to copy the contents of the report directly from the screen and paste it into a different format.

Once you have accepted your answers, you will be able to download a **text version** of your questions and answers. You will accept your answers in the evaluation tab that we will explain a few sentences down.

You have the option to download the contents as a **CSV** file that is intended to be loaded into other programs for reporting.

The **mobile option** allows you to send the contents of the report to your mobile application, although some setup is required.

Open report provides in on-screen version of the report in a PDF file format, which can be **sent via email**, as long as the environment settings are complete with in your BAP framework.

The **evaluation button** enables you as the recipient of the interview to modify your answers, as well, to accept the answers once they are correct. When taking an interview that is part of a BAP strategy, there will be multiple interviews. Once you have completed and accepted one interview, you will be prompted to proceed to the next interview. Remember. Once you have accepted your answer as correct, you can no longer modify that answer. Your answers are saved upon entry, so start and stop the interview process to meet your priorities and work style.

Act

1. For the sake of this book, we will choose the checkbox next to the simplified report.

Let's go ahead and check your work. The bapValidator reviews your entered information with the objectives for your submission established by the creator of the bapInterview which is accomplished via key phrases.

You have completed the 4.2.3 identification, authentication, and access control-1 interview, congratulations.

4.2.3-identification, authentication, and access control. Question #1
Does the system support federal user authentication via CAC/PIV credentials? [IA-2(12)]
Yes

How?
We have established an LDAP server in addition to our AD Server. They are both clustered for high availability.

Documentation:
Yes. We have detailed documentation at \FPC1\FISMACert\

Interview:
During the interview, we validated that the LDAP and AD servers are functional. We recommend that the site uses BAP to add continuous monitoring to establish the control strength in real-time.

☑ Simplified Report (Download Text) (Open Report) (Send Report) (Evaluation)

Insight

Illustrated on this page is an example of the **simplified report**.

Act

1. For this book, we will choose the **evaluation** button.

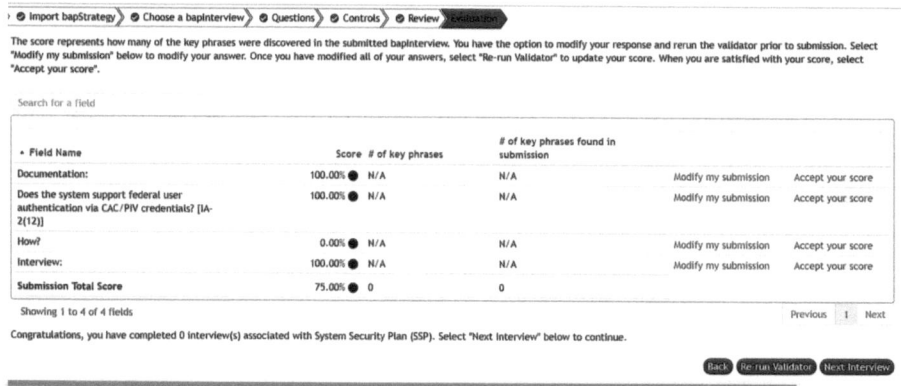

Insight

Note that all of the scores are 100% with the exception of the **"how?"** field? The column titled **"# of key phrases found in submission"** there is an N/A. This N/A indicates that no key phrases have been associated with the text question: "how?".

Why do we have a 0% if there are no key phrases?

Remember that a text box question/answer can leverage key phrases, in addition can be validated to confirm that the answer is not empty.

Act

1. Choose **"Modify my submission"** on the **"how?"** line/row.

Modify your answer for How? question.

How?

We have established an LDAP and AD server in the environment.

Insight

Note in the illustration above that we of answered the question of how?

Act

1. Complete information and choose "**save**".

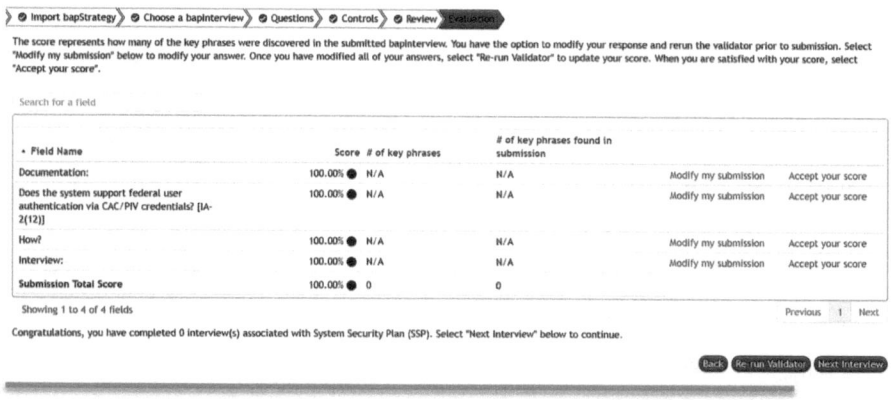

Congratulations, you have completed 0 interview(s) associated with System Security Plan (SSP). Select "Next Interview" below to continue.

Insight

This is a review screen to show the results of the changes we have made. We modified the submission for the question "**how?**". Note that the score is now 100% because the answer was added to the question. We selected "**rerun validator**" and validation changed from 0% to 100%.

Act

1. Choose "**rerun validator**" following any modification to an answer.

2. To continue to the next interview in the strategy file, either choose "**next interview**", or choose from the horizontal menu "**choose a BAP interview**". If you choose "next interview", the software will randomly select an interview that has not been completed. Whereas, if you choose "choose a BAP interview" you will be able to select the interview you wish to complete.

Name of the bapinterview to search for

▴ bapinterview Name	Last Modified	Status
4.2.3 identification, authentication, and access control-1 v1 by Jeffrey Lush	10/19/2018 17:07	Accepted
4.2.3-identification, authentication and access control-2 v2 by Jeffrey Lush	10/19/2018 17:07	Not started
4.2.3-identification, authentication, and access control-4 v1 by Jeffrey Lush	10/19/2018 17:07	Not started
4.2.3-identification, authentication, and access control-5 v1 by Jeffrey Lush	10/19/2018 17:07	Not started
4.2.3-identification, authentication, and access control-6 v1 by Jeffrey Lush	10/19/2018 17:07	Not started
4.2.3-identification, authentication, and access control-7 v1 by Jeffrey Lush	10/19/2018 17:07	Not started
4.2.3-identification, authentication, and access control-8 v1 by Jeffrey Lush	10/19/2018 17:07	Not started
4.2.3-identification, authentication, and access control-9 v1 by Jeffrey Lush	10/19/2018 17:07	Not started
4.2.4-audit, alerting, malware, and incident response-1 v1 by Jeffrey Lush	10/19/2018 17:07	Not started
4.2.4-audit, alerting, malware, and incident response-2 v1 by Jeffrey Lush	10/19/2018 17:07	Not started

Showing 1 to 10 of 66 bapinterviews   Previous 1 2 3 4 5 6 7 Next

Insight

Illustrated is a review screen of the results we've produced in this chapter. Note the interview, in the far right column under "status", the interview has been "accepted", indicating that the recipient of the interview has completed and accepted all answers.

Act

1. Continue to complete interviews.

Chapter eight

Review bapInterview results

bapApps Center
import bapStrategy
export bapStrategy
import bapValidate
export bapValidate
bapValidate
my bapCheck
org bapCheck
bapReader
bapReader Processes
demo ControlKP
demo EventKP
demo QuickCheck
wizard bapStrategy
bapRemediate
bapRemediate Report

Insight

There are two options to check interviews that have been completed. You can modify answers if they have not been accepted, run reports, etc.

"**My bapCheck**" allows you to view the interviews that you personally have taken on your BAP framework.

"**Org bapCheck**" is the organizations results of the interviews that have been taken.

Act

1. For this book, we will work with the example of "**My bapCheck**". Please choose "**My bapCheck**".

- bapinterview Name	Last Modified	Status
4.2.3 identification, authentication, and access control v1 by Jeffrey Lush	10/19/2018 03:20	Finished
4.3.4-continuous monitoring capabilities-4 v2 by Jeffrey Lush	10/19/2018 03:22	Finished
SC-13 CRYPTOGRAPHIC PROTECTION_interview v1 by Jeffrey Lush	10/03/2018 15:00	Finished

Insight

As illustrated above, we can choose any past interviews.

Act

1. Choose the first interview.

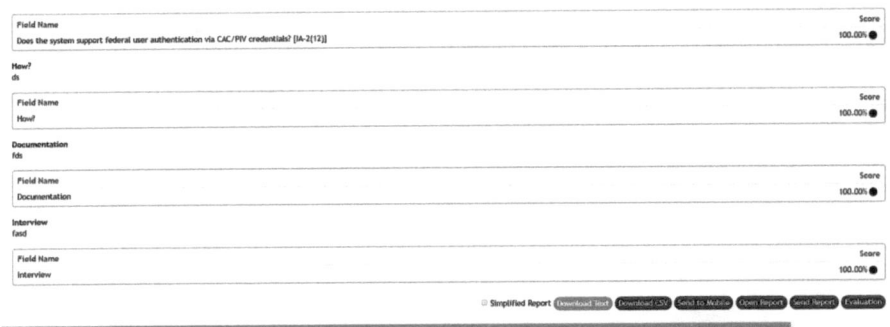

Insight

As explained in the previous chapter, scores are presented to assist the originator and the recipient of the interview to understand the validity of the answers provided.

Act

1. For the sake of following along in this book, choose **"evaluation"**.

- Field Name	Score	# of key phrases	# of key phrases found in submission		
Documentation	100.00%	N/A	N/A	Modify my submission	Accept your score
Does the system support federal user authentication via CAC/PIV credentials? [IA-2(12)]	100.00%	N/A	N/A	Modify my submission	Accept your score
How?	100.00%	N/A	N/A	Modify my submission	Accept your score
Interview	100.00%	N/A	N/A	Modify my submission	Accept your score
Submission Total Score	100.00%	0	0		

Showing 1 to 4 of 4 fields

Previous 1 Next

Re-run Validator Close

Insight

Aas explained in the previous chapter, you can modify and accept your scores.

Act

1. Modify/accept your scores as desired.

Glossary

bapValidate, also known as

bapValidate (when consumed)

Establishing standards requires the collection of information, and
bapValidate performs that task. bapValidate can be accessed
from within the component builder for the team members that
are developing the interviews. For the consumption of the
bapValidate, is obtained through the BAP apps center as
bapValidate, as well as in the BAP QuickStart menu.

bapControl, also known as

cybersecurity control

cybersecurity standard

A standard often referred to as a control which is made up of a stated
objective and the implementation of processes and technolo-
gies to meet that objective. Within the cybersecurity industry
this is referred to as a security control, although can be applied
to any number of standards implemented within an organization. bapControl is hosted by the BAP Component Builder and
allows organizations to add new, edit, merge, allocate and associate BAP Controls with specific policies.

bapAI ControlKP, also known as

control KP

as discussed, a control includes an objective and the implementation
of processes and technology to meet the objective. A unique
BAP attribute allows an organization to align real-time threat
to established standards. To accomplish this, the bapAI ControlKP is the collection of key phrases (KP) and their
associated weights. This information is used as a valuation cri-
terion for the artificial intelligence (AI) running within the
bapFramework. The bapAI ControlKP component allows you

to create and modify the assigned key phrases to specific standards or bapControls. The bapAI ControlKP is found within the BAP Component Builder.

KP, also known as

Key phrase

A key phrase is in the expression or definition of a standard or event within the organization. Key phrases interpret technical language or industry jargon into natural language. Key phrases are found within any BAP components that leverage the BAP artificial intelligence (bapAI).

Component also known as

slot

A component of the bapFramework is a sub process to achieve a specific task within the bapFramework. Components are created by subject matter experts, general users, and prepackaged components available for download from the bapMarketplace. BAP components fit into a BAP slot.

BAP slot, also known as

a BAP component

The BAP slot enables BAP components to run within the bapFramework. BAP is built upon an open framework, allowing components to be allocated as slots to provide specific services. A bapControl, for example, on encryption is required to meet a business objective. The bapControl that enables encryption is established in a slot. Slot licenses are imported using the bapFramework import menu, whereas the management of the slots is found within the tools menu of the bapFramework. Slots can be purchased through the bapMarketplace.

bapAI EventKP, also known as

event KP

Understanding real-time threat detection requires the use of event logs and traps. The event logs are populated with specific event codes and key phrases. The interpretation of the event codes and their relationship to the multiple standards within the environment is accomplished within the bapAI EventKP. The bapAI EventKP works in conjunction with the bapAI ControlKP to establish near real-time threat. The bapAI EventKP can be managed using the component builder.

bapBaseline

security policy

A bapBaseline is a collection of standards to meet specific organization and business objectives. The BAP standard provides a consistent collection of standards that are often applied to multiple baselines or policies. The objective of this standard stays consistent, although the implementation of the standard may vary depending upon the policy. The BAP Component Builder enables organizations to create, edit and manage their baselines and policies. Each bapBaseline consumes a single slot although the variance of the policy specific implementation of the slot consuming standard does not consume a slot as it is specific to the policy. The impact of a specific standard as it relates to specific policies is adjusted using priorities within the development of the bapBaseline.

BAP QuickCheck

BAP QuickCheck is a simple tool that allows users to enter in three key phrases and search up to three documents at a time. BAP QuickCheck is found within the bapApps Center as well as bapsolution.com. BAP QuickCheck illustrates the strength of the BAP artificial intelligence, without all of the detail associated with bapReader and bapValidate. Following a successful QuickCheck, BAP provides the number of times a specific keyword and key phrase was discovered within the selected documents BAP QuickCheck is a free BAP tool that is part of the bapFramework.

bapVisual

bapVisual hosts the dashboard and reports.

Process baseline

The process baseline function is part of the tools menu within the bapFramework. Process baseline allows organizations to establish policies and test the policies in real time for effectiveness.

Ideas about your Strategy

Please continue to use this space for ideas about your strategy…

Please continue to use this space for ideas about your strategy...